S. No-well! No-well! No-well!

A.

T. No-well! No-well! No-well!

B.

S. No-well! No-well!

A.

T. Ho - di - e, Ho - di - e Christ - us nat - - us est:_____
  *Christ - mas Day, Christmas Day, Christ was born_____ on Christmas Day._____

B.

S. No-well!_____

A.

T. Ho - di - e, Ho - di - e sal - va - tor ap - pa - ru - it:_____
  Christ - mas Day, Christ - mas Day, Our Sav - iour was born on Christ - mas Day._____

B.

*The English words may be sung at the discretion of the conductor, but the composer would much prefer the Latin.

This Day (Chorus)

6

This Day (Chorus)

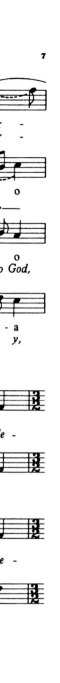

8

10

Christ - us nat - - - us est:____
Christ was born____ on Christ-mas Day.____

Christ - us nat - - - us est:____
Christ was born____ on Christ-mas Day.____
No-well!

No-well! No-well! No-well!____ No-well! No-well! No-well!

____ No-well!____ No-well! No-well! No-well!____

____ No-well!____ No-well! No-well!____ No-well!

____ No-well!____ No-well! No-well!____ No-well!

II NARRATION

[TREBLES STAND: CHORUS REMAINS STANDING]

IV NARRATION

[T. & B. STAND : S. & A. REMAIN STANDING]

V CHORAL

[CHORUS REMAINS STANDING]

VI NARRATION

[CHORUS REMAINS STANDING]

will, good will, good will to-ward men, good will to-ward men,___ good will,___

___ good___ will to-ward men.___ Good_____ good___ will to-ward

men.___ Glo - ry to God_____ glo - ry to God in

We___ praise thee, we_ bless thee, we___ wor-ship thee, we

the high-est, glo - ry to God_ in the high-est, in the high - est.

glo-ri-fy thee, we give thanks to thee for__ thy great glo - ry:

This Day (Chorus)

22

This Day (Chorus)

VII SONG
[CHORUS SITS]
[TREBLES SIT]

TACET

VIII NARRATION
[TREBLES STAND]

* A few voices from the back rows

IX PASTORAL

[TREBLES SIT]

TACET

X NARRATION
[TREBLES STAND]

But___ Ma - ry kept all these_ things,___

and pon-dered them_ in her heart.___

XI LULLABY
[CHORUS S. & A. STANDS]

Sweet was the song the Vir - gin

sang When she to Beth - lem Ju - da_ came And was de -

- liv - ered of a son, That bless - ed Je - sus hath to name.___

"Lul - la,

lul - la, lul - la-bye,___ lul - la, lul - la, lul - la,

"Lul - la, lul - la, lul - la-bye,___

XII HYMN

[CHORUS S. & A. SIT, TREBLES SIT]
TACET

XIII NARRATION
[TREBLES STAND]

heard that they de - part - ed;___ and lo!___ the star, which they saw in the East,

went be - fore them___ till it came and stood ov - er where the young child

was,___ When they saw the star, they re - joiced___ with ex - ceed - ing

great_ joy.___ And when they were come in - to the house,_____ they saw the young child__

_ with Ma - ry his_mother, and fell_down and wor-shipped him: and_

when they had o -pened their_ trea-sures, they pre - sent-ed un - to him gifts;___

gold,_____ and frank - in-cense and myrrh._____

XIV THE MARCH OF THE THREE KINGS
[CHORUS STAND]

king - doms of wis - dom sec-ret and far____ Come Cas - par, Mel-chi -or,

Bal-tha - sar;___ They ride through time, they ride through night Led by the star's fore -

30

This Day (Chorus)

Attacca
subito No. XV

XV CHORAL
[CHORUS REMAINS STANDING]

Str.
Harp

S.
is that mak - eth night; Let no mur - mur nor rude wind
an - gels dance in flight; Joy of heaven shall now un - bind

*Verse 1 to be sung by a Semi-chorus of from 8 to 16 voices (in this
verse boys' voices are not to be used); 2nd Verse to be sung full.

XVI EPILOGUE
[CHORUS REMAINS STANDING]

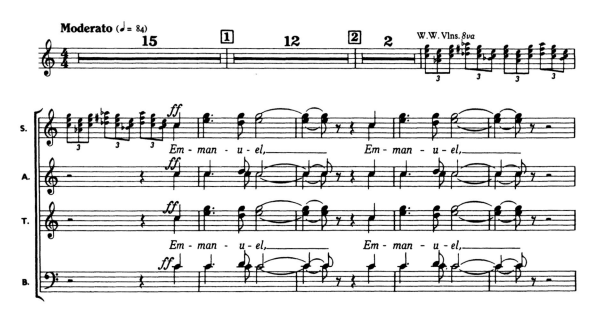

*Note : ♩ ♩ ♩ a shade slower than ♫♫ of No. III